polari plays

Published by Polari Plays, an imprint of Polari Press.

polari.com @polaripress

ISBN: 978-1-914237-14-0

First published in the UK in 2023.

Copyright © Alistair Hall, 2023 under exclusive licence to Polari Press Ltd. Alistair Hall has asserted his right under the Copyright, Designs and Patents Act, 1988, to be identified as author of this work.

Cover design and typesetting by Peter Collins for Polari.
Typeset in a custom typeface by Bijou Type and Roslindale by
David Jonathan Ross. Cover photograph by Jamie Luke Scoular.

Printed on responsibly sourced paper using vegetable inks.
Polari Press is committed to reducing its environmental impact.

Polari Press does not have any control over, or responsibility for, any third-party websites referred to in this book. All internet addresses given in this book were correct at the time of going to press. The author and publisher regret any inconvenience caused if addresses have changed or sites have ceased to exist, but can accept no responsibility for any such changes.

No rights in incidental music or songs contained in the work are hereby granted and performance rights for any performance/presentation whatsoever must be obtained from the respective copyright owners.

All rights whatsoever in this play are strictly reserved and application for performance etc should be made before rehearsals by emailing contact@polari.press. All professional/amateur production enquiries should be made to them. Permission must be sought whether the title is presented for charity or gain and whether or not admission is charged. No alterations to the text or title are permitted without the author's prior written consent. Both Polari Press and the playwright welcome applications for amateur productions and public readings.

No part of this book may be reproduced, stored in a retrieval system, or transmitted in any form, by any means, not known or yet to be invented, including mechanical, electronic, photocopying, recording, videotaping, or otherwise, without the prior written permission of the publisher.

A catalogue record for this book is available from the British Library.

To find out more about our authors and work, visit polari.press and sign up to our newsletter.

alistair hall

declan

Presented at the Edinburgh Festival Fringe,
Underbelly Cowgate, 15–27 August 2023.

First performed at Camden People's Theatre,
29 November – 3 December 2022:

Written & performed by Alistair Hall
Director & Dramaturg Billy Barrett
Lighting Designer Amy Daniels
Sound Designer Jamie Lu
Technical Stage Manager Eliott Sheppard

cast & creative team

ALISTAIR HALL
Writer and performer

Alistair was born in Chippenham, Wiltshire and now lives in London. He graduated from RADA in 2019. *Declan* is his debut play. *Declan* is a recipient of the inaugural Keep it Fringe Award set up by the Edinburgh Fringe Society and Phoebe-Waller Bridge. The play was also shortlisted for the Bristol Old Vic and Pleasance Partnership Award. Alistair's acting credits include *Family Tree* (Actors Touring Company); *Safe* (Norwich Theatre Royal); and *Rose Pandemic* (BAFTA Crew).

BILLY BARRETT
Director

Billy is a director, writer, and co-artistic director of the devised theatre company Breach. Recent productions directed for Breach include the verbatim musical *After the Act*, about Section 28, and the courtroom drama *It's True, It's True, It's True*, about the baroque painter Artemisia Gentileschi. Other work as a director includes Tabby Lamb's *Since U Been Gone*. He has led workshops in documentary and devised theatre for organisations including the National Theatre, Old Vic and the

Roundhouse. As a visiting director he has worked at drama schools including RADA, LIPA and Guildhall.

JAMIE LU
Sound Designer

Jamie is a London-based scenographer and sound designer. Theatre credits as sound designer include: *Going for Gold* and *Road* (Chelsea Theatre); *Mother's Day* and *Grills* (Camden People's Theatre); *Burnout* (R&D, Vault Festival and tour); *Still Here* (Jack Studio Theatre); *Hedda Gabler* (Reading Rep); *Smoke* and *Tokyo Rose* (Southwark Playhouse); *Iphigenia* (Hope Theatre); *Nanny* (R&D with Folio Theatre); *Fester* (R&D with Halfpace Theatre); *A Gig for Ghosts* (Soho Theatre); *The Apology*, *We Started to Sing* and *Broken Lad* (Arcola Theatre); *Paradise Lost* (Shipwright); *The Unicorn*, *What the Heart Wants* and *How to Build a Wax Figure* (Edinburgh Fringe 2022); *Sorry We Didn't Die at Sea* (Seven Dials Playhouse); *The Blue House* (Blue Elephant Theatre); *Dirty Hearts* (Old Red Lion). As assistant sound designer: *Henry V* (Donmar). Jamie was also sound designer for the audio play *The Dream Machine* (Fizzy Sherbet).

AMY DANIELS
Lighting Designer

Amy is a London-based lighting designer and occasional production manager. Theatre credits as lighting designer include: *The Life & Death of All of Us* and *Mother's Day* (Camden People's Theatre); *Rise* (Kiln Theatre); *There Was a Little Girl* (VAULT Festival); *Cell Outs* (Traverse Theatre/Pleasance Theatre); *No Place Like Home* (Pleasance Theatre). As production/technical stage manager: *Welcome Home* (Soho Theatre); *Human Jam* and *If You Love Me This Might Hurt* (Camden People's Theatre).

ELIOTT SHEPPARD
Technical Stage Manager

Eliott is a freelance stage manager. Having trained at Bristol Old Vic Theatre School, his recent credits include *Family Tree* (UK tour); *The Elephant Song* (Park Theatre); *Cinderella* and *Sleeping Beauty* (The Maltings, Ely); *Salt* and *I Can't Hear You* (Theatre503); *Fritz & Matlock*, *All By Myself* and *Bloody Mary* (Edinburgh Fringe 2022); *Jane Eyre* (Minack Theatre); *We Are Here* (Bush Theatre); and *The Isklander Trilogy* (Swamp Motel).

acknowledgements

Created with the support of Camden People's Theatre, Bristol Old Vic's Ferment programme, London Performance Studios, RADA, Edinburgh Fringe Society and The Forward Trust. With special thanks to Ian Morgan, Alexis Gregory, Rae Clarke, Sean Vickers, Martin Moriarty, Rob Nowill, Hynam Kendall, Lou Stoppard, Jon Williams, Peter Collins, Alastair Curtis, Patrick Waugh, Jamie Luke Scoular, Lucy Hunt, Chris Power, and everyone who has supported *Declan*.

I never sat down and planned to write this play. It sort of happened by accident. I'm worried that sounds pretentious, but it's true.

I was in an improvisation class at RADA in 2018. I was training on the MA Theatre Lab course which provided its students with a highly experimental year of actor training, devising, and left-field performance making. In this particular class, we'd all been asked to improvise a monologue whilst in a headstand.

Upside down with my legs held in the air, a story about a lonely man living in a small Wiltshire town began to fall out of my mouth. He was watching a vampire loiter outside of his bedroom window. I heard my classmates laughing and then going silent as the monologue got darker. It became a tense cat and mouse thriller between the man and the vampire.

As I spoke, I felt the beginnings of the character Jimbo. The strange, oddball essence that makes him such a loveable outsider. I kept that momentum going after class. I developed the character of Jimbo and ended up presenting a scratch version of *Declan* as an exam piece.

In October 2019, just a few weeks after my dad died of cancer, I performed a work-in-progress sharing of *Declan* at Bloomsbury Theatre as part of the Bloomsbury Festival.

In June 2020, I presented a filmed version of the play online. This was directed by Alexis Gregory and produced by the Actors Centre (now Seven Dials Playhouse). It was the height of the pandemic and many of us were switching to digital performances after having live production runs slashed due to lockdown.

This digital run gained a strong audience who reacted with interest and intrigue. As the world started to open up again and the theatre industry went back to normal (ish) I put the play down and focused on new things.

In early 2022, during one of those rough unemployment periods actors so often go through, my partner Billy Barrett—a director and dramaturg—suggested I revisit *Declan*. The idea was to give it the live audience outing it never had, and expand it into a fully-realised piece.

In November 2022, I finally performed *Declan* in front of an audience. It ran for five nights at Camden People's Theatre. As I write this, I am preparing to debut the play at the Edinburgh Fringe. *Declan* finally feels as if it has been developed in all the right ways. The many tweaks and changes have helped make it a short, but crafted, piece of theatre that should hover over its audience long after the lights go down.

Declan is a play about Jimbo, an outsider trapped in a small rural town. It follows his obsession with his best friend Declan, who has gone missing. As the story unfolds we hear about Jimbo's life of neglect and abuse, and how he uses his imagination to escape. We also get to fall in love with Jimbo's strange sense of humour. He wears an eccentricity I've come to recognise in so many fellow Wiltshire folk.

There isn't one writing session, rehearsal, or performance where I haven't thought about my dad, Kenny. A sensitive, caring and troubled man who really did the best he could with the mind he had. Jimbo's track in the world of *Declan* is the same. He is trying to survive.

Declan is inspired by some of my experiences growing up in Chippenham, a small market town in Wiltshire. Back in the late nineties and early noughties, it wasn't a particularly welcoming place for gay teenagers like me. Just like Jimbo, I was spat on, had stones thrown at my head and was called every homophobic name or slur there was going.

And then there was the Section-28-induced silence at school. I don't remember any sex education classes at all let alone a dialogue about relationships or intimacy in the LGBTQ+ community.

Although these experiences have nurtured the roots of the play, most of Jimbo's story is fictional. So much of what happens to Jimbo has not happened to me. This includes the abuse he suffers at home and his surreal, nightmarish visions.

Despite the heavy themes of the play, there has been so much love in every rehearsal. Working with my partner Billy has been a total joy. He is one of the most sensitive, emotionally in-tune and freeing directors I have had the pleasure of working with. His creative vision is extraordinary. The level of detail he has helped provide this short play is inspiring.

When I think about the heart of *Declan*, I see the streets of a small town that never felt like home to me. I see my dad as a younger man in his thirties. I wonder if this is when his struggles with mental health began. I wonder what life was like for other people in the town, queer or not, struggling with their heads and feeling unable to talk about it.

This play is dedicated to the memory of my dad, Kenny, but it's also very much for my wonderful mum, Adele, my siblings, Ann-Louise and Luis, Uncle Jim and Aunty Karen, and my entire extended family from Wiltshire. They have always and only ever encouraged me.

Just a few weeks before I sat down to write this, Chippenham hosted its first ever Pride Festival. LGTBQ+ flags were dotted all over the town and the event provided a day of joy for the local queer community. I saw signs in pub windows showing allyship with the event, there was a march and a concert.

Chippenham now even has its first gay mayor.

He's called Declan.

Alistair Hall, 2023

Declan

by Alistair Hall

A one-person play

Setting and staging

The play is set in a small Wiltshire town.
In a hollow family home.
By a polluted canal.

Dingy, desolate, damp.

The character of **JIMBO** *is childlike, erratic, funny, fragile and haunted.*

Through his recollections we meet:

KIDDY

DECLAN

COLLIE

MUM

DAD

NAN

MRS FEENEY

BAZ

MRS HUNT

MISS DAY

And **KING EDWARD II**

The text has been stripped of stage directions to allow for individual interpretation.

The play is performed under a single hanging lightbulb. The bulb flickers to indicate scene transitions or in response to moments in the play.

The performer carries a plastic bag filled with a handful of props. Each prop represents an item of emotional importance mentioned in the text.

A soundscape underscores the play.

The audience should feel locked in with **JIMBO**.

Notes on the text

A line break during dialogue indicates a renewing of speech.

An em-dash (—) denotes an interruption.

Lines in quotation marks indicate **JIMBO** *speaking as another character.*

Lines in italics indicate **JIMBO** *coming out of direct address to the audience and speaking to another character or to himself.*

Content warning

Contains references to homophobia, suicide and child abuse.

4

Kiddy

JIMBO This is quite difficult for me, actually. Cos he was drinkin' it. He was drinkin' my blood. To be honest, I didn't think he'd actually drink my blood. Course I didn't. Didn't think he'd drink it from my neck, my arm or my bum. But he did.

I dunno what I was expectin'. I'd seen him in the street outside my house. This Kiddy. The minute the sun went down and the moon went up—***boom!***—there he was. Like clockwork. I didn't think nuffin' of it at first. He weren't exactly up to much. Not really. He'd walk up and down the pavement. Really starin' down at it. Sometimes he'd stop and lean against a lamppost. He'd light a fag and blow smoke into the air. I'd watch him from my bedroom window.

I remember tryin' to figure out what this Kiddy was all about. What sorta mood he was in, y'know? He had a cap on though and hung his head low so I couldn't see his face. He didn't seem happy. Or sad. Just sorta. Well, nothin' really. But then it all started to happen.

One night he showed up as normal but somethin' were different. The streetlights above him flickered on and then off. On and then off. He weren't doin' no pacin' up and down this time. No sparkin' up a ciggy. He just stood and watched. Me.

I tried to step back from the window and pretend I weren't lookin' but it were pointless. He'd clocked me. He started raisin' his hand. I thought he was gonna give me a wave but he took his cap off, lifted his head high and—
Oh.
Wow.
He looked like my mate Declan. Bit greyer in the face, mind but same floppy brown hair, same big brown eyes.

And then he was crossin' the street. Slowly at first but then he picked up his pace. He never took his eyes off me. The minute I went downstairs and leaned into the peephole, he was already there. At my front door.

He started knockin'. Just, like, quite normal at first but the more I left him hangin' the more impatient he got. I could hear his knuckles pressin' against the wood, his breathin' was gettin' harder and then he started kickin' and—
Alright, you can come in.

Dunno why I said it. Didn't want him to but the next thing y'know my hand was reachin' down for the handle and I just...

He pushed right past me and barged into the hallway.
'Scuse me.
'Scuse me you can't come in 'ere like that.
I said you can't come in 'ere like that!

His eyes changed from brown to red. And he licked his lips at me. And then I dunno how he done it but he started makin' me lead him upstairs to my bedroom. I felt all light. My arms and legs were like clouds.
It's just to show him.
I'm just showin' him.
That's what I kept tellin' myself.

I turned my bedroom light on and oh my god, he started screamin'. So I turned the light off. We were standin' in the dark and it was so awkward. I could feel him lookin' at me. Really lookin' at me like he couldn't keep his eyes off me. He asked me to take my clothes off.
Nope.
He asked again.
No.
He asked again.

No!

Then he hissed at me.

No, really. He hissed, like a—

HISSSSSSSSSSS!

Alright, calm down.

And so I took my clothes off.

He went quiet then. Didn't move. Didn't even breathe. Just this long—quite painful if I'm honest—silence. I felt like he was disgusted by me.

He started walkin' around me. Circlin'. He knelt down behind me and I could feel his hands touchin' the backs o'my thighs. I could feel him sniffin' me. Really sniffin'. Like a doggy. And I could feel him lookin' at it. Really lookin' at it. And then he bit it. He bit my bum.

That felt like gettin' a tattoo but much deeper. And I could smell meat like steak before it's cooked. And he felt so cold against me. My skin felt cold. And he was drinkin' my blood. Felt like a fish suckin' on me. So fuckin' weird.

He grabbed my shoulders and flipped me into a headstand. He held my legs in place. He was lookin' down at me. He wasn't sayin' nuffin'. I wasn't sayin' nuffin'. Mute. Then he made a gruntin' noise. Like a piggy. **_Oink oink!_**

I like farm animals, I do. So I thought, fuck it. I'm just gonna ask him.
Do you like farm animals?
But he bit my ankle. I felt his teeth rip through my flesh and wrap 'emselves 'round the bone and I could smell meat again.

Then I remembered I was still wearin' socks. Declan's socks. The ones he used to love. I could still feel 'is feet in 'em. I never took 'em off. This gave me an idea.

Hang about!
My socks have somethin' they wanna ask you.
'Scuse me.
I Said.
My.
Socks.
Have.
Somethin'.
They.
Wanna.
Ask.
You.

Have you seen my mate Declan?

But he just grabbed me, chucked me against the wall and knocked me out.

Declan

JIMBO I was best mates with Declan for one whole year and then he went missin'. Literally, one minute he were there and then he were just gone. Murder, suicide, kidnap. I considered all of it. He said he was takin' my dog Collie for a walk but he didn't come back. All I found was his trainers and socks down by the canal. I found Collie nearby though. Alive!

Declan and me were tight from the moment we met. I'd spent my whole life bored by most people. Not bored in a rude way just bored in a stop chucklin' and pointin' at me kinda way. There were these twats at school. They saw somethin' in me they didn't quite take to. They laughed, prodded, laughed, prodded, poked and laughed s'more. They followed me round like a pack'o wolves.

There was this teacher I quite liked though. Miss Day. She had shiny blonde hair and dressed like a lady out o'one of them fashion magazines. She wore pink jumpers and knee-high boots. The way she took care of herself reminded me o'my mum. I liked it.

I remember one mornin', those twats were singin' their dawn fuckin' chorus o'laughter at me. I'd 'ad enough. I went to class early and sat at my desk. I weren't really one for cryin' much but I couldn't help myself. Three tears came down my face. One hit my hand, the other hit my lap, and the other sunk right down to my shoe.

Miss Day came up behind me. Put her hand on my shoulder. She knelt down beside me and asked if everythin' were okay. I told her to open the window. She trotted over to it and the minute she pulled the handle down that laughter poured into the room.

They do it all day long.
'*I know,*' she said. '*I know.*'
Will you make 'em stop?
'*Let me see what I can do.*'
She knelt back down beside me.
I felt like I could talk to her.
I don't wanna laugh like 'em.
Be like 'em.

I sorta feel—
Well, I just don't think I'm like that.
Like they are.
I don't get it.

Miss, I think maybe I'm—
She put her hand on my arm.
'Let's stop there, Jimbo.'

She pulled away. Said she'd speak to the headmaster. Everyone else turned up for class and that were that. She ended up doin' fuck all to help me. I hated Miss Day after that. Started skippin' her class instead.

That's how it went. I ditched her class, started skivin' some others until eventually I didn't bother goin' to school at all. Even after I got expelled and started workin' different jobs in town, I didn't really, y'know, click with no-one. I just couldn't seem to do it. Some people were really nice. They'd chat to me about their girlfriends, boyfriends, or kids, but my mind just sorta drifted.

With Declan it were different. He kept me on my toes. We weren't even that alike or nothin', not really. Well, he couldn't seem to keep a job down either but he looked different, sounded different to me and to everyone else round here.

When my dad gave me money to get a dog, it were Declan who helped me pick Collie out from the animal shop. She were only little. Half Border Collie, half somethin' else. She had one blue eye, one brown one, and a limp, bless her. I walked her every day.

Whenever I felt like crap, Declan knew how to snap me out of it.

'Just think about bein' somewhere new,' he'd say.
I dunno. Where?
'Swindon. Or maybe you could go to Bath?'

Truth is, I didn't know what any of those places looked like. Whenever I thought about bein' somewhere else my mind just went sorta blank.

I caught Declan wankin' once. I did. He said he needed a place to stay for a few days so I told him he could kip in my room.
Just come at night and don't let my dad see you.
I woke up to this sheet shufflin' sound.
That's when I saw him.
'Come and give me a hand if you want.'
No, I don't do that!

The night Declan went missin', I were pissed off cos he hadn't been to see me since that 'appened.
S'not that I didn't wanna give 'im a hand.

I did.

I really did.

I just didn't know how to do that.

On myself I did.

O'course I did.

Just not on someone else.

Not on Declan.

I'd wanna get it right.

Y'know?

And part o'me felt guilty.

About wantin' to do it at all, let alone do it right.

I shoulda just talked to him.

We were tight.

But I didn't.

And he left.

In the middle o'the night.

It weren't like him to go quiet on me.

To stop callin' round for me.

I was upset and thought maybe he didn't wanna be friends no more.

I was in the kitchen havin' a chat with Collie about it and th—

Alright Declan.

Oh. Fine. I'll just get her lead for you.

Collie!

You can take her down to the canal.

And we could have some dinner when you get back if you like.

Right. Okay. Well, bring her back soon. She's already had a walk today.

And they said it's gonna rain.

Wait... Declan...

I...

Collie's really missed you.

Tap Tap Tap

JIMBO *Oi Dad, what exactly was it about her that you didn't like?*
'Ey?
I thought you'd like her.
Long legs, blue eyes, pink ring on her finger.
Yeah, it's plastic but it looks like a—
I dunno. A gem.
She's perfect.
Well, she was till you stamped on her 'ead.

I don't understand what's so wrong with buyin' you a Barbie doll.
She was pretty. Like Mum. I thought she'd remind you of Mum.
You coulda played with her.

I was in Woolies lookin' for sweets and I saw it.
Her. I saw her.
She had the little dress on and those shoes and I thought it looked just like Mum.
Don't you think that's mad?
She's the spittin' image of her.

I wanted to do somethin' the way you do.
With my hands.
And arms.
So, I thought I'd pick this Barbie up off the shelf, buy it,
and give it you.

I notice you spendin' all your spare time in 'ere.
Washin' up and wipin'.
Door closed.

D'you reckon we could go somewhere?
Get out of this house.
Go on a little adventure.
Even if it's just for a day.

You said you'd take me to see Edward II.
Where's he buried. Over in Gloucester.
That's not far. Can you drive us there?
Show me his grave.
We could dig him up.

I like him, I do.
As a king.
Miss Day done a class on him.
Told us about him gettin' booted off the throne and executed.
Then everyone started sayin' he was a faggot.

'A right royal faggot!'

She said, 'Stop it.'

'But he is, ain't he, Miss?'

She said, 'Do you know what that word means? Hey?
Do you?'

'Oooooh.'

Everyone went silent.

Miss Day never mentioned him again.

I bought a film about him from the video shop though.

I was meant to be rentin' A Bug's Life *but there it was.*

Starin' down at me from the shelf.

A whole film about King Edward II.

It were on sale.

One pound.

I been watchin' it every single night.

I keep the volume down low.

King Edward don't wear many clothes in it.

He loves another bloke.

Gaveston.

And there's snakes and smoke and fights.

I keep pressin' rewind, rewind, rewind.

I can't seem to look away.

You ever had that, Dad?

Your eyes, heart and stomach all pulled in the same

direction?

I have to force myself to press stop, turn it off and go to bed.

There was a tappin' at my window the other night.

tap

    tap

        tap

Musta been past midnight because the house was quiet as.

You were quiet.

Lights out.

I got woken up by it.

All that tappin'.

I lied down for a bit just listenin' but then I thought it could be Mum comin' home.

I pulled the curtain back, as you do, but there was nobody there.

No-one.

Nothin'.

Dad?

You listenin'?

Oi.

Alright, fine.

Is this...

Is this because I got you a Barbie?

Mrs Feeney

JIMBO After that Kiddy knocked me out, I woke up and he were gone. The blood stains on my carpet were gone. The smell o'meat – just gone. The front door were locked even though he didn't 'av a key. That's magic. It is.

When I'd asked Kiddy outright if he'd seen my mate Declan, he flipped out. Somethin' in me was tellin' me he knew exactly where he was. So, I decided to go lookin' and find out. I went knockin' on every door on my street I did.

Number forty.
Alright Baz.
He always wore the same T-shirt.
KEEP ENGLAND ENGLISH
He couldn't breathe without his little machine on wheels. Normally I'd 'av a bit o'sympathy but the truth is I didn't like Baz.
He kept a load o'dogs locked up in his garden shed.
You could hear 'em barkin' and beggin' for fresh air.
'Don't mind those lot. I'm gettin' 'em ready for a fight.'
Right. Okay.
Baz, I was actually wonderin' if you'd seen this lad.

'What lad?'

He's like about my height.

Wears a cap.

'No. Sorry son. That don't ring no bells.'

Alright, fine. See ya!

Number 42.

Ello?

Ello?

Dunno know why I bothered.

Mr and Mrs Hunt never answered the door. Not to no-one.

Mr Hunt was always comin' and goin' in his fancy car and Mrs Hunt was a right old snob.

I heard shufflin' behind the door.

Alright, it's Jimbo.

'Ello?

I was wonderin' if you'd seen this lad.

He's scruffy.

Light brown eyes.

Mrs Hunt I know you're there. I can actually see your feet.

Look, this Kiddy, he's been 'angin' round loads lately.

I heard some more shufflin'.

Heard her goin' up the stairs.

A door closed.

Mrs Hunt?

Fine! Fuck you!

Number 45.
Alright, Mrs Feeney. How you doin'?
She had rollers in her hair, fag on, and old fluffy cat slippers.
No, thanks, you know I don't.
I was actually wonderin' if you'd seen this lad who's been hangin' round.
He broke in and bit me. Sucked my blood.
She stubbed her fag out on the carpet.
Then she looked at me funny.
'Oh lovey, you ain't been right since your mum went.
Why don't you come in for a cuppa?'
I can't. I gotta find him.
'You ain't got time for a tea w'me? Now that's not very neighbourly, is it?'
She touched my wrist.
Alright, fine. Go on then.

That house adn't seen a hoover in years.
It were like sniffin' dust.
Framed pictures of her family covered in grey snow.
Carpets so powdery my feet sunk into 'em.
She patted down her favourite photo of Mr Feeney.
'He always 'ad the time o'day for you. Said you were the

sweetest little lad he'd ever known.'

Nobody ever found out exactly what happened to Mr Feeney.

She calls herself a widow but rumour has it he left town with his special friend Kevin.

She lit a fresh ciggy.

'You sure you don't want one, darlin'?'

Nope.

'You could stay for dinner? I'll do yer favourite. Chips and beans.'

I really can't. I need to find him.

'Fine. Suit yourself.'

She seemed angry w'me.

Then she nestled in really close and looked me right in the eye.

'I have seen this Kiddy you're on about.

Yeah. Course I have.

He was down by the canal.

Right where your mate Declan went missin'.'

Fucker

JIMBO That year with Declan was fuckin' quality.

He was silly as hell and that made me take it all a bit less seriously.

Life.

With him, I could just take it on the chin a bit y'know?

He'd call for me like we were school mates or somethin'.

I knew he'd come for me cos I'd hear him whistlin' down the end o' my driveway.

That was my cue to go and join 'im.

To see what the day had to offer us.

Literally all we'd do is muck about.

Leg it up to the big field up at the end o' town.

A long dry stretch o'land that looked bleached in the summer.

You could see the motorway in the distance.

All those exits.

Cars makin' their way t'Melksham.

Trowbridge.

Bristol.

Bath.

Somerset.

Declan told me to walk close to him.

Side by side.
Our fingers would touch and my skin buzzed from it.
First time that happened, I pulled away.
I went red in the face and looked about to see if anyone were watchin' us.
He didn't care though.
He put his fingers back by mine.
Played music out his Sony Ericsson.

And we'd walk. And walk. And walk. Mostly round in circles cos the field weren't that big.
But with him it felt like infinity.
We'd go on and on and on.
Come the end of an afternoon every inch o' that land had our footprints on it.

Sometimes we'd go back to mine and Declan would make me play kisses with him.
We'd jump around on my bed and take it in turns seein' how many we could blow at each other.

Kiss one	Kiss two
Kiss three	Kiss four
Kiss five	*Stop movin'!*

Six	Seven
Eight	Nine
Ten	*It hurts my lips!*
Eleven	Twelve
Kiss	Kiss
Kiss	

Once we played for a whole evenin'.

I was covered in 'em.

Kisses.

I liked it.

'*Come here,*' he said.

So, I started to shuffle down to him.

Everythin' slowed down and I felt all slurry.

My cheeks felt warm.

Could feel bits of sweat down my back.

He looked so calm and I dunno – comfy.

He pulled me close to him and I could smell his neck.

My fingers started tracin' his jaw and then his lips and then we...

We snogged.

My first time.

It felt amazing and we cuddled each other and I could smell his deodorant blending into mine and we started jumpin' again and then—

'Jimbo, what the fuck are you doin' up there?!'

Shit! He's home!

Uh... Nothin' Dad!

I looked round the room for Declan.

I saw the window was open.

He'd done a runner.

Fucker.

He was always doin' it.

Just dissappearin' on me like that.

Fucker.

I didn't mind though.

Not really.

He made me laugh, he did.

And he always came back t'me.

Whistlin' down the end o'my driveway.

Callin' for me.

Always.

A Love Letter

JIMBO *Mum, I'm thirteen years old and standin' in between the house and the bottom of the garden. It's rainin' but it's sunny. I can smell cut grass. Cut grass and cow shit. I touched myself today, I did. I been doin' that loads lately. My hand is all sticky from it. Sticky like when I help myself to more jam. That kinda sticky.*

When my hand is down my pants I do think about girls but I think about boys too.
Their arms.
Chests.
Dicks.
No. Girls.
Tits tits tits.
Oh, but boys...
Boys.   Boys.   _{Dicks.}   Boys.

I think about the girls and the boys at school but then I remember I been gettin' stones thrown at the back of my head. It happens when I walk into town, on my way round Nan's and sometimes here in my own garden. If they don't have stones they lob spit over the fence. They make it rain on me. Call me limp-wristed.

Weirdo.

Bender.

I hear 'em chucklin' in my sleep.

Where did you go, Mum?

Dad calls it your vanishing act.

You should come home.

You should.

Even if you don't actually come into the house.

You could stand outside.

Next to me.

Get your brolly out.

Open it up over my head.

Stop all the stones and spit from fallin' down on me.

Please.

I'll hear you shufflin' in through the gate.

And maybe you will come into the house.

Through the back door.

You'll be home.

As if you never went away.

As if you climbed down out of the sky.

And…

And you'll doll yourself up like you used to.

Yeah.

Lipstick.

You'll take me into the kitchen and we'll both wear aprons.

Radio on.

Dancing round the oven.

We'll get dizzy.

And when Dad doesn't come home, we'll just ignore it.

So fuckin' dizzy.

You'll say it's bed-time again.

Take me upstairs.

Close my bedroom door behind us.

You'll make sure it's shut good and tight.

I'll say Mum, I reckon I'm gettin' too old for this n—

'Ssssssh.'

You'll lie down next to me.

Stroke my hair.

Ear.

Neck.

Chest.

Belly button.

Thighs.

And then your hand slides—

Front door.

Then you'll stop.

It's Dad.

We'll hear him hang his coat up.

Crack open a tinnie.

Light a fag.

And you'll take your hand back and say, 'N'night.'

You won't even look at me.

You'll just close the bedroom door behind you.

I'll be lyin' there alone.

Wide awake.

I'll think about the girls and boys at school chucklin' away.

Nope.

I don't wanna see their faces.

And I don't think I wanna see yours, Mum.

I wanna see—

I dunno.

Anyone else.

Anyone.

So, I'll roll over.

Squeeze my eyes shut and try and sleep.

Nan's Birthday

JIMBO The night I met Declan, everything changed for me. It was my first time leavin' the house in weeks. I'd get like that sometimes, y'see. I'd lock myself up. I felt like the town was closin' in on me and I had to hide. Sounds daft, don't it? It's true though.

Anyway, that night I'd forgotten I had somewhere to be.
I was tucked away thinkin':
They're right, they are.
'There he is! Big weirdo!'
That's what I've become.

Then Nan appeared with a balloon with the number ninety on it.
'Come on. It's my party tonight. Gonna need you there my love.'
She stood me in front of my bedroom mirror.
'Let's pop a shirt on you.'
She found one and buttoned it up. Right to the top.
'You're a good lookin' fella, aren't you? In your own funny kinda way.'
She tapped me round the back of the head.
I wanted to ask her somethin'.
I reckon she knew what I wanted to ask.
Does Dad ever talk to you about Mum?

But I didn't ask.
I just patted my shirt down and smiled.
She looked at me through the mirror.
'C'mon now. You can't keep hidin' like this.
You're a man.
You ain't supposed to be sweet.
Now let's go 'av some fun.'

For Nan's party, Dad decided to go really big and make a fuss. He rented out the top floor of Illusions, the local nightclub. He invited a load of people. I didn't know half of 'em to be honest. There was a DJ. Dad gave me a job, though. Told me to look after the buffet.
I had to check we had plenty of everythin'.

Crisps ✓
Fanta ✓
Coke ✓
Diet Coke ✓
Sausage rolls ✓
Veggie sausage rolls ✓
Mini pizzas ✓
Cakes ✓
Box o' red wine ✓
Box o' white wine ✓
Box o' pink wine ✓
A bottle of voddy for Nan ✓

I was making a plate of food for myself and—

Alright.

Yeah, help yourself.

You can use a plate, y'know.

I don't drink. Not allowed.

What's your name then?

Declan.

Nice.

No. Just tonight.

It's my nan's party. She's ninety.

How come you're—

Oh, right.

What?

I can't dance.

No, I actually can't dance. I can't just leave the buffet.

No, I don't do everythin' I'm told.

Sod it.

Go on then.

God, you're a good dancer.

I'm not copyin' you!

Alright, I am.

We can't.

Not here.

Follow me.

'Don't even fuckin' think about it!'

Dad. I'm only dancin'.

'Not tonight. Don't show your nan up!'

Dad.

'You're a not kid, Jimbo!'

Dad, you're embarrassin' me.

'I'm embarrassin' you?!'

SLAP

'I dunno what to do with you anymore!'

Sorry Declan, I can't dance with you tonight.

Canal One (Hunter)

JIMBO After Mrs Feeney said she'd seen him, it turned into a right old hunt. It were Kiddy who'd taken Declan. I was sure of it. I went home, lay on my bed and waited for nighttime. Fingers twitchin', eyes blinkin'. I couldn't stay still. I 'ad to calm myself.

Right.
What would my Declan do?
He'd put his hand over mine.
Warm.
That's nice.
Keep it there.
He'd tell me to breathe steady.
'*In.*
Out.
In.
Out.
Now close your eyes and calm the fuck down.'
So that's what I did.

>   Duvet   Pillow
>   Warm   Fuzzy   Noddin'
>   Nice... Nice... Nice.
>   Off...

Awake!

I saw the moon through my window.
It's time!

I shot up out o' bed. Flew downstairs. I grabbed
Collie's lead. C'mon girly. I legged it down to the canal.
The neighbourhood whizzin' past me. My heart was
thumpin' so hard. It was thumpin' in my mouth.

I'm comin' for you!

The streetlights flickered on and then off. On and then
off. Kiddy were tauntin' me. Like he knew I were comin'.

I remember hearin' the canal before I saw it. That sound
o'water tricklin' down by the bridge. I looked up into the
trees. And then I were there. Right where Mrs Feeney
said she'd seen him. Right where my Declan went missin'.

Oi!
C'mon then.
I've got some more blood for you.
Oi!
C'mon.
I know you're here, Kiddy.
Bark!

Collie, ssh!

Oi!

Bark!

Collie!

C'mon!

I heard a rustlin' up above.

A branch snapped and fell on my head.

Collie! Collie! Come back!

I heard more rustlin'.

And then—

Fuckin' hell.

I saw him.

Kiddy.

He were like...

Like...

Hoverin'.

Hoverin' down to me.

And then these words just fell out my mouth:

You stole him from me.

I know you did.

My best friend.

Declan.

Show me where he is.

Show me where he is now or I'm gonna smash your fuckin' 'ead in!

Coronation

JIMBO *Dad, what exactly was it about her that you didn't like?*
'Ey?
You musta loved her at some point.
Long legs, blue eyes.
You put a ring on her finger.

What made everythin' go tits up?
When did she start chattin' away to herself?
Starin' through the walls.
Lyin' on the livin' room floor grinnin' up at the ceilin'.
Runnin' away from the phone every time it rang.
The dancin' in the middle o' the kitchen.
D'you know I didn't mind that.
I liked that.
Havin' a dance w'my mum.
Radio on.
Dancin' round the oven light.

I remember the three of us sat round the telly watchin'
Blind Date.
I was only a little'un and I were askin' questions.
Who's that? What they doin'? Why they all sat on stools?
I was hearin' all this talk o'love.

Seein' couples on the screen.

Bloke.

Lady.

Together.

Bloke and lady.

I remember lookin' back at you and Mum.

You 'ad yer arms round each other.

Round me.

And we felt tight.

Like a…

Well, like a family.

But that memory don't really mean shit anymore does it?

'Ey?

You listenin'?

When did it start to turn?

This house.

Turn over on itself and hollow out into this shit show.

'Ey?

You took all the photos down off the wall.

You act like she never fuckin' slept, ate, raised a kid in 'ere.

I can't stand it.

There was a tappin' at my window the other night.

tap

    tap

        tap

Musta been past midnight because the house was quiet as.

You were quiet.

Lights out.

I got woken up by it.

All that tappin'.

I lied down for a bit just listenin' but then I thought it could be Mum comin' home.

I pulled the curtain back, as you do, and someone were there but it weren't Mum.

Nope.

It was him.

King Edward II.

Just floatin' at the window.

He looked proud.

Bit tired and pale mind but still proud.

The crown on his head was sparklin'.

I'd never seen anythin' like it.

All shiny and golden with bits o'soil on it.

Do you wanna come in, Edward?

He laughed at that.

Shook his head no.

Is it true?

What they said about you in class?

Oi.

You don't say much do you?

He took his crown off.

Just like that.
As if it were light as a feather.
And he put it on my head.
I felt so tall and proud.
Just like him.
And then he was off.
Bye Edward!
I slept in that crown, I did.

Dad.
I don't need you to drive me to Gloucester no more.
I don't need you to take me to see Edward II.
Cos I already seen him.
He dug himself up for me.

Meat Factory

JIMBO Declan and me would hang out on the roof of
Strings, the local chippy. He never wanted nothin' to eat
but I'd buy myself a veggie burger and chips and then
we'd go round the back. He'd give me a leg up the wall
and we'd climb onto the roof.

Our feet would dangle over the edge and the smell of
vinegar would waft up into the air. There was a girl who
worked at Strings, she had a swan tattoo down her arm
and she kept duckin' out for fag breaks.

We'd watch people comin' and goin'. The man with five
battered cods and a never endin' pile of chips bagged up
ready to go. There was this pregnant woman who came
in for a can of Tango and that's it. Just a can of Tango.
Orange flavour.

One time I spotted Nan walkin' in to buy herself some
dinner. I went to shout down to her but Declan grabbed
my hand. Put his finger over my lips. I didn't care if she
saw us though. Or Dad. After the bust-up at Nan's party,
I tried to steer clear of Declan but it weren't happening.
He always showed up. He liked to hang out about under

the street lights. Sometimes he'd jump the fence and stand in my garden. He'd stare up at the house.

With Declan time just flew and flew, right. Up on that roof, my feet hangin' next to his, I felt like an actual person. More alive than on any birthday, more alive than when Nan gave me my Christmas prezzies or when I woke up in the mornin's and I could feel myself throbbin' down below.

Declan laughed at me for havin' veggie burgers, he did. He asked me why I didn't eat meat and I decided it was time to tell him about the meat factory.

That's where Dad worked when I were little.
The meat factory's not its proper name but that's what we all called it.
It's where all the cows go to die.
We went inside once. Me and Mum.
It was Dad's birthday and Mum wanted to surprise him after his shift.
She started gettin' ready.
She smudged lippy across her mouth and made her hair big and curly.
She put her favourite red dress with the front pockets on but it were backwards.

'Mum it's the wrong way round,' I said but she just pouted in the mirror.

She was excited to surprise Dad.

She got like that sometimes.

The blacks of her eyes went big like saucers and she'd be chewin' her mouth off.

We drove to the meat factory and when we walked in I noticed some of the men who worked with Dad were lookin' at us funny. They were starin' at Mum like she'd done somethin' wrong.

'He can't go in there,' someone said and they grabbed me by the shoulder and held me back but I could see into the factory through a gap in the door. Mum went on in.

I saw the back of her walkin' into a row of hangin' cows. They were upside down with no skin and their bones were stickin' out.

It looked like it 'ad been rainin' blood in there.

Mum's hips swayed as she disappeared.

I heard her singin' to Dad.

'Happy birthday to you.

Happy birthday to you.

Happy birthday dear—'

SLAP

Mum screamed.

Dad was fumin'.

'You can't keep carryin' on like this. Yer off yer head. I'm not playin' this game no more. Pretendin' I dunno what you been doin' to him. It's not right.'

Next thing y'know, Mum was draggin' me back to the car. Her cheek was as red as her dress and she was shakin'.

I watched her starin' ahead as she drove.

I don't think it was the road she was lookin' at.

Her eyes gazed over the other cars like somethin' else were pullin' her forward.

'Shall we do some kitchen dancin' when we get home Mum?'

That's when I felt the back of her hand smack me across the face.

'Get out. Just get out.'

She made me walk all the way home.

Took me ages.

Mum didn't come back that night.

Or the next.

Or the next.

Or the—

Vanishing act.

After that I didn't touch meat.

Dad would come home with his bags from the factory but I stopped askin' what was in 'em.

He'd cook steak for dinner and I'd refuse to eat it.
He tried burgers and sausages. All of it.
I said no.
So, that's why I like veggie burgers.

Declan put his arm round me then.
His flesh softened round mine.
My nose 'gainst his neck.
The sky went dark blue and then black.

Canal Two (Ending)

JIMBO *You stole him from me.*

I know you did.

My best friend.

Declan.

Show me where he is.

Show me where he is now or I'm gonna smash your fuckin' 'ead in.

Kiddy's floating above me like a fuckin witch. His eyes are changin' colour again. Light brown to red. Light brown to red. Oh my god, I wanna run away. Find Collie and get out of here but I can't move. My body's like a sack o' cement and my hands are clenched tight.

Kiddy raises his hand.

I shrink, close my eyes.

But he don't hit me.

He starts leadin' me—

Leadin' me down to the edge o' the water.

I look at Kiddy and suddenly he looks normal.

Like he means no harm.

Not to me or to anyone else for that matter.

You look just like him, you do.
My Declan.
I've wanted to tell you that since the first night I saw you.

He's laughin' at this.
Pointin' down at his feet.
He's wearin' Declan's trainers.
I look at his face again.
Same big brown eyes, same floppy brown hair.
Oh my god. It's you.
I wanna go and hug him.
Declan.
But his face twists.
He turns into the others.

Tim...
        ...and then Aaron...
        ...becomes Simon...

                ...Keith
                Russell...
                ...Toby
                Mikey...
                ...Freddy
                Winston...

And I can hear Dad shoutin' in my ear.

'Pack it in, Jimbo. Pack it in!'

Robbie　　　Jonny　　　Al　　　Jake　　　Kev

'Not one o' these lads is fuckin' real.'

Rich　　　Liam　　　Ted　　　Mark　　　Francis
　　　　　　　　…and Declan

My Declan.

Out of all them, you feel the most proper.
You feel…
Really - r e a l l y - real.
Look at you.
Beautiful.
But I think it's time for you t'clear off now.
All o'you.
Go on.

And now she decides to show up.

I hear her walkin' behind me.

I turn and look at her.

Wet skin, blue lips, red dress.

Pockets stuffed with stones.

Mum, I think we need to have words.
First you love me too much and then you do yourself in.
Bit harsh not to leave a note.
I woulda liked that.
To see your squiggly handwritin' one last time:

I'm so sorry. Love Mum. Xx

Ah well.
It's all over now.
You can't follow me no more.
Not today, not ever.
I'm movin' on.
Takin' myself off somewhere nicer.
And you can't come.

Next thing y'know I'm up to my neck in that canal water. Fuckin' freezin'. I'm shiverin' but then again, when aren't I? I've spent my whole life scared o' people and places but now I'm washin' 'em all off me. Washin' all of that shite away.

I see my face lookin' back at me through the water.
Got quite a smile on me, I have.
I think I look quite nice.
Don't think I look weird at all.

I think about my town.

The people in it.

Mrs Feeney windin' me up tellin' me she could see who I saw.

I really thought she could.

I reckon she'll miss me.

        I think about Collie.

        Her little bark.

        Nan.

        Dad.

        Their love.

        But that house.

        That fuckin' house.

Someone do us a favour and burn it to the fucking ground.

I hold my breath.

I let that water slip right over my head.

My arms are movin, legs kickin', eyes openin', and I'm divin' down deep.

I see a plastic bag.

A cow's head.

A bag o'chips.

All wet now.

Barbie's leg.

A sausage roll.

And then I see it.
A little flash o'light.
It's singin' to me.
And I'm swimmin' towards it till I can touch it.
All shiny and golden with bits o'soil on it.
And it's his crown.
King Edward's.

Well, it's mine now actually.

I'm thinkin' about the motorway by the edge o'town.

All those exits.

Cars makin' their way t'Melksham.
Trowbridge.
Bristol.
Bath.
Somerset.

I'm gonna be alright you know.

I am.

Blackout.

Polari Press

Taking our name from the secret slang Polari, we are an independent publishing house that seeks out hidden voices and helps them be heard.

Although Polari was spoken almost exclusively by gay and bisexual men, the nature of clandestine meetings of the mid-1900s, when homosexuality was still criminalised, brought together people from all walks of life who all had an influence on the language.

Cockney, Romany, and Italian languages mixed with the colloquialisms of thespians, circus performers, wrestlers, sailors, and wider criminal communities to create a slang to express their sexuality secretly and safely.

Inspired by these origins, we publish queer voices as well as other marginalised groups, to share our perspectives with each other and help build a collaborative platform for all of us.

polari.com

Polari Plays

We are creating an active archive for queer-authored play scripts and performance.

For a complete listing of Polari Plays titles, visit:
polari.press/plays

Follow us on social media:
@PolariPress